To Teach as Jesus Did

A Pastoral Message on Catholic Education

November 1972
National Conference of Catholic Bishops

ISBN 1-55586-063-X

1973
United States Catholic Conference, Inc.
1312 Massachusetts Avenue, N.W.
Washington, D.C. 20005-4105

Contents

TO TEACH AS JESUS DID

A Pastoral Message on Catholic Education

Preface

1 This pastoral message is the product of wide consultation involving many individuals and groups. It reflects a painstaking effort to obtain the views of persons from a variety of backgrounds and interests—priests, religious men and women, lay people, professional educators at all levels of education, parents, students. Much of this consultation took place at the national level but even more occurred at the local diocesan level, where bishops sought out the views of the people regarding various drafts of the document. While, in the last analysis, the pastoral represents the views of the American bishops and only they are responsible for what it says, grateful recognition is due the indispensable contributions of all those who participated in the collaborative effort involved in its preparation, itself in many ways a model of the shared responsibility for educational ministry which the document envisions and warmly recommends.

2 The pastoral is also written against the background of the Second Vatican Council's *Declaration on Christian Education* which requested national hierarchies to issue detailed statements on the educational ministry considered in the context of the Church and society in their own countries.

3 The pastoral's scope is broad but not all-encompassing. A virtually endless catalogue of programs, institutions, and activities could be gathered together under the rubric of "education." It was therefore necessary to employ some principles of exclusion to avoid producing a treatise of excessive length and, perhaps, superficiality. This document is concerned in the main with those agencies and instruments under Church sponsorship which are commonly recognized as "educational" by professional and layman alike and through which a deliberate and systematic effort is made to achieve what are commonly recognized as "educational" objectives. This is not to discount the educational/formational role played by communications media, liturgy—indeed one of the most powerful and appropriate educative instruments at the disposal of the Church—and countless other familial, social, and pastoral efforts, but only to state that they could not be considered in depth in this particular document. In addition, some extremely important educational programs are not treated here because they have already received detailed attention by the bishops elsewhere (e.g., the education of priests, which is the subject of the National Conference of Catholic Bishops' recently published *Program of Priestly Formation*).

4 As the concluding section of this document states, the pastoral is not to be regarded as the "final word" on its subject on either the theoretical or practical level. It will serve a useful purpose if it proves a catalyst for efforts to deal realistically with problems of polarization and of confusion now confronting the educational ministry. Thus one hopes that the ideas it contains will be studied closely, criticized intelligently, and, where possible, implemented successfully. In the years ahead American Catholics should continue to articulate and implement their commitment to the educational ministry in ways suited to their times and circumstances. Within both the Christian community and the educational ministry the mission to teach as Jesus did is a dynamic mandate for Christians of all times, places, and conditions.

I. TO TEACH AS JESUS DID

5 *"Lord," said Thomas, "we do not know where you are going. How can we know the way?" Jesus told him: "I am the way, and the truth, and the life; no one comes to the Father but through me. If you really knew me, you would know my Father also. From this point on you know him; you have seen him." (John, 14:5-7)*

6 Proclaiming the Gospel is a perennial task and joy for the Church of Jesus Christ. Rarely if ever has it been more pressing a need, more urgent a duty, and more ennobling a vocation than in these times when mankind stands poised between unprecedented fulfillment and equally unprecedented calamity.

7 Catholic education is an expression of the mission entrusted by Jesus to the Church He founded. Through education the Church seeks to prepare its members to proclaim the Good News and to translate this proclamation into action. Since the Christian vocation is a call to transform oneself and society with God's help, the educational efforts of the Church must encompass the twin purposes of personal sanctification and social reform in light of Christian values.

8 Thus one crucial measure of the success or failure of the educational ministry is how well it enables men to hear the message of hope contained in the Gospel, to base their love and service of God upon this message, to achieve a vital personal relationship with Christ, and to share the Gospel's realistic view of the human condition which recognizes the fact of evil and personal sin while affirming hope.

9 Christian hope is of special importance today when many people express a naive optimism which fails to admit the reality and effects of sin upon the individual and society, and when many others, fully aware of evil in themselves and society, are tempted to indulge in crippling despair. In face of these two attitudes the Church can make a unique contribution by preaching the Gospel of hope. The Gospel proclaims the dignity and freedom of each person and gives assurance that men are right to hope for personal salvation and for the ultimate conquest of sin, isolation, injustice, privation and death because these evils have already been conquered in the person of Jesus Christ.

10 The success of the Church's educational mission will also be judged by how well it helps the Catholic community to see the dignity of human life with the vision of Jesus and involve itself in the search for solutions to the pressing problems of society. Christians are obliged to seek justice and peace in the world. Catholics individually and collectively should join wherever possible with all persons of good will in the effort to solve social problems in ways which consistently reflect Gospel values.

11 Since special knowledge and skills are needed for the effective pursuit of justice and peace, Christian education is basic to the effort to fulfill the demands of the Gospel in many different communities: family, church, neighborhood, working world, civic arena, international scene. To discern the practical demands of justice is often difficult. Yet Christians must be prepared to perform these difficult tasks of discernment; social needs "must in the years to come take first place among (their) preoccupations." (Pope Paul VI, *A Call to Action*, 7)

12 The Church is an instrument of salvation and a sign of Christ in the world today. His mission is the Church's mission; His message is the Church's message. Jesus was sent to reveal the deepest truth about God and at the same time reveal "man to himself and make his supreme calling clear." (*The Church Today*, 22) He commissioned His Church to do the same; to teach men and women about God and themselves, to foster their love of God and one another.

13 Education is one of the most important ways by which the Church fulfills its commitment to the dignity of the person and the building of community. Community is central to educational ministry both as a necessary condition and an ardently desired goal. The educational efforts of the Church must therefore be directed to forming persons-in-community; for the education of the individual Christian is important not only to his solitary destiny but also to the destinies of the many communities in which he lives.

14 The educational mission of the Church is an integrated ministry embracing three interlocking dimensions: the message revealed by God *(didache)* which the Church proclaims; fellowship in the life of the Holy Spirit *(koinonia)*; service to the Christian community and the entire human community *(diakonia)*. While these three essential elements can be separated for the sake of analysis, they are joined in the one educational ministry. Each educational program or institution under Church sponsorship is obliged to contribute in its own way to the realization of the threefold purpose within the total educational ministry. Other conceptual frameworks can also be employed to present and analyze the Church's educational mission, but this one has several advantages: it corresponds to a long tradition and also meets exceptionally well the educational needs and aspirations of men and women in our times.

MESSAGE

15 *"For I have not spoken on my own; no, the Father who sent me has commanded me what to say and how to speak. Since I know that his commandment means eternal life, whatever I say is spoken just as he instructed me." (John, 12:49-50)*

16 Revelation is the act by which God unfolds to mankind the mystery of Himself and His plan for salvation. In Jesus, the Son of God, the message of the Old Law was fulfilled and the fullness of God's message was communicated. At the time of the Apostles the message of salvation was completed, and we therefore "await no further new public revelation before the glorious manifestation of our Lord Jesus Christ." (*Divine Revelation,* 4) It is this message, this doctrine, which the Church is called to proclaim authentically and fully.

17 This does not preclude development in doctrine, properly understood, or change in the forms in which it is expressed. The tradition handed on by the Apostles is a "living tradition" through which God continues His conversation with His people. God "still secretly directs, through the Holy Spirit, in sacred tradition, by the light and sense of the faith, the Church, His bride, and speaks with her, so that the People of God, under the leadership of the magisterium, may attain a fuller understanding of revelation." (*General Catechetical Directory,* 13) There is, then, a growth in understanding of the message which has been handed down. (*Divine Revelation,* 8)

18 In proclaiming all things which His Father commanded Him to reveal, Jesus used images from the lives of His hearers and

spoke in the idiom of His day. The Church, too, must use contemporary methods and language to proclaim the message of
Christ to men and women today. The proclamation of the message is therefore "not a mere repetition of ancient doctrine."
(*General Catechetical Directory*, 13) Furthermore, within the
fundamental unity of the faith, there is room for a plurality of
cultural differences, forms of expression, and theological views.
But what is taught and how it is expressed are subject to the
magisterium, the teaching authority of the Church, as guarantor
of authenticity.

19   The teaching Church calls upon each of us to have an active
faith in God and His revealed truth. Under the influence of the
Holy Spirit, man gives total adherence to God revealing Himself.
Faith involves intellectual acceptance but also much more.
Through faith men have a new vision of God, the world, and
themselves. They must not only accept the Christian message
but act on it, witnessing as individuals and a community to all
that Jesus said and did. Catechesis thus "gives clarity and vigor
to faith, nourishes a life lived according to the spirit of Christ,
leads to a knowing and active participation in the liturgical mystery, and inspires apostolic action." (*Christian Education*, 4)

20   In sum, doctrine is not merely a matter for the intellect, but
is the basis for a way of life as envisioned by St. Paul: "Let us
profess the truth in love and grow to the full maturity of Christ
the head." (Ephesians, 4:15)

COMMUNITY

21   *"I give you a new commandment: Love one another.*
Such as my love has been for you, so must your love be
for each other. This is how all will know you for my
disciples: your love for one another." (John, 13:34-35)

22   As God's plan unfolds in the life of an individual Christian,
he grows in awareness that, as a child of God, he does not live
in isolation from others. From the moment of Baptism he be-
comes a member of a new and larger family, the Christian community. Reborn in Baptism, he is joined to others in common
faith, hope, and love. This community is based not on force or
accident of geographic location or even on deeper ties of ethnic

origin, but on the life of the Spirit which unites its members in a unique fellowship so intimate that Paul likens it to a body of which each individual is a part and Jesus Himself is the Head. In this community one person's problem is everyone's problem and one person's victory is everyone's victory. Never before and never since the coming of Jesus Christ has anyone proposed such a community.

23 Community is at the heart of Christian education not simply as a concept to be taught but as a reality to be lived. Through education, men must be moved to build community in all areas of life; they can do this best if they have learned the meaning of community by experiencing it. Formed by this experience, they are better able to build community in their families, their places of work, their neighborhoods, their nation, their world.

24 Christian fellowship grows in personal relationships of friendship, trust and love infused with a vision of men and women as children of God redeemed by Christ. It is fostered especially by the Eucharist which is at once sign of community and cause of its growth. From a Christian perspective, integral personal growth, even growth in grace and the spiritual life, is not possible without integral social life. To understand this is a high form of learning; to foster such understanding is a crucial task of education.

25 In the family children learn to believe what their parents' words and example teach about God, and parents enrich their own faith by participating in the formal religious education of their children: for example, by preparing them to receive the Sacraments of Penance, Eucharist and Confirmation. The members of a parish grow in fellowship by coming together to worship God and by making a shared response of faith on occasions of joy and stress. Creating readiness for growth in community through worship and through the events of everyday life is an integral part of the task of Catholic education, which also seeks to build community within its own programs and institutions.

26 Our nation, blessed by God with enormous resources, has a heavy responsibility in the larger community of people on this planet. Christian educational ministry includes as a dimension of high importance the education of our own people to the imperatives of justice which should direct our national political, military, cultural and economic policies. In the absence of justice no enduring peace is possible. Thus the teaching of recent Popes, the Council and the Synod of Bishops concerning peace and justice for all nations and peoples must be communicated effectively and accepted fully. In this task we invite the collaboration of mission-sending societies whose apostolate includes educating American Catholics regarding their international responsibilities.

SERVICE

27 *"You address me as 'Teacher' and 'Lord,' and fittingly enough, for that is what I am. But if I washed your feet —I who am Teacher and Lord—then you must wash each other's feet. What I just did was to give you an example: as I have done, so you must do."* (John, 13:13-15)

28 The experience of Christian community leads naturally to service. Christ gives His people different gifts not only for themselves but for others. Each must serve the other for the good of all. The Church is a servant community in which those who hunger are to be filled; the ignorant are to be taught; the homeless to receive shelter; the sick cared for; the distressed consoled; the oppressed set free—all so that men may more fully realize their human potential and more readily enjoy life with God now and eternally.

29 But the Christian community should not be concerned only for itself. Christ did not intend it to live walled off from the world any more than He intended each person to work out his destiny in isolation from others. Fidelity to the will of Christ joins His community with the total human community. "Thus the mission of the Church will show its religious, and by that very fact, its supremely human character." (*The Church Today,* 11) No human joy, no human sorrow is a matter of indifference to the community established by Jesus. In today's world this requires that the Christian community be involved in seeking solutions to a host of complex problems, such as war, poverty, racism, and environmental pollution, which undermine community within and among nations. Christians render such service by prayer and worship and also by direct participation in the cause of social reform.

30 It is imperative that the Church render the service of educational ministry today. Many institutions in society possess much larger material resources and thus can do far more to meet the material needs of man. None, however, has the unique resources of vision and values entrusted to His community by Jesus Christ. To suppose that the Church's mission of service is somehow less urgent in today's world than in the past is to fail to recognize mankind's enduring spiritual need and the unique capacity for meeting that need possessed by the Christian community.

———

31 Beyond question the vision of the threefold educational ministry presented here is an ambitious one. Were it of human origin, one might well despair of its attainment. But since it represents God's plan, it must be energetically pursued.

32 Even now it is being realized in many places. All three aspects of the educational mission are present, for example, in a well organized, comprehensive parish program of education where the teaching of authentic doctrine supports and is supported by the building of community, and teaching and fellowship in turn support and are supported by Christian service through sharing spiritual and temporal goods with those in need. In such a parish Catholic education's lessons are learned in classroom and pew; yet not only there, but also in the experience of living in a Christian community of faith actively engaged in service of God, Church and neighbor.

II. A WORLD IN TRANSITION:
FAITH AND TECHNOLOGY

33 Underlying virtually all of the changes occurring in the world today, both as instrument and cause, are technology and the technological worldview. Technology is one of the most marvelous expressions of the human spirit in history; but it is not an unmixed blessing. It can enrich life immeasurably or make a tragedy of life. The choice is man's, and education has a powerful role in shaping that choice.

34 Technological progress equips man with sophisticated means of communication, analysis and research. The speed and ease of travel, the marvel of instantaneous communication via satellite, television and telephone, the "transistor revolution" which carries new information and ideas to the most remote corners of the earth—these and many other developments foster growth in awareness that the human family is one, united though diverse.

35 Scientific tools of research and analysis like the computer have created a knowledge explosion. The past itself is more accessible to people and they are able to understand it far better than before. Thus not only does the present generation of mankind experience powerful influences toward unity but its bonds with earlier cultures also grow stronger. In this context the continuity of God's living revelation and of teaching based on the enduring deposit of faith is more apparent; the beauty of God's plan for community among all His scattered children can be more readily appreciated, and the plan itself can be more easily realized.

36 On the other hand, one must acknowledge a distressing paradox: this same technology threatens the unity and even the future of mankind. Its instruments destroy ancient patterns of life and uproot peoples from their traditions and history. Values cherished for centuries are abruptly challenged, and the stability of the social order is weakened if not destroyed. If this generation is, as some suggest, moving into a new era of global culture, it simultaneously risks losing the values of particular cultures which deserve to be preserved.

37   Although technology can create unparalleled material prosperity for all men, its abuse can be a tool of human selfishness. At present, technologically advanced nations are accumulating wealth at a rate which widens the gap between themselves and the poor nations of the world. The same phenomenon—a tragic gulf between rich and poor—is also present within many technologically developed nations, including our own. Our readiness for sharing has not kept pace with our skill at acquiring.

38   Technology poses new threats to the dignity of the person. It makes possible violence and destruction on a scale hitherto undreamed of. In our own nation's wealthy society the immense output of goods and services too often distracts its citizens from awareness of their duty to God and their fellows, without satisfying their deepest needs for stability, friendship and meaning.

39   Faith suffers in the resulting climate of uncertainty and alienation. Torn between the appeals of idealism and reform on the one hand, and the seductions of greed and self-indulgence on the other, many people drift on the surface of life, without roots, without meaning, without love.

40   Yet profound human needs endure, and the educational mission of the Church must use old ways and new to meet them. This task is more difficult today than at many times in the past, precisely because turbulence and uncertainty bring with them skepticism toward the institutions of society, including those of the Church. In evaluating and responding to this contemporary phenomenon, it would be a serious mistake to identify mere externals with essential faith, or to confuse rejection of what is merely familiar with repudiation of our basic heritage. This underlines the need for balanced discernment in place of simplistic solutions.

41   Faithful to the past and open to the future, we must accept the burden and welcome the opportunity of proclaiming the Gospel of Christ in our times. Where this is a summons to change, we must be willing to change. Where this is a call to stand firm, we must not yield. In this spirit, our discussion turns now to the concrete forms and structures of the educational mission.

III. GIVING FORM TO THE VISION

1. THE EDUCATIONAL MINISTRY TO ADULTS

42 The Church's educational mission takes form in many different programs and institutions adapted to the needs of those to be educated. We shall first consider those directed to adults, including in this category both adult or continuing education and also the various forms of the ministry in higher education.

ADULT EDUCATION

43 Today, perhaps more than ever before, it is important to recognize that learning is a lifelong experience. Rapid, radical changes in contemporary society demand well planned, continuing efforts to assimilate new data, new insights, new modes of thinking and acting. This is necessary for adults to function efficiently, but, more important, to achieve full realization of their potential as persons whose destiny includes but also transcends this life. Thus they will also enjoy ever deepening fellowship within the many communities to which each of them belongs. Consequently the continuing education of adults is situated not at the periphery of the Church's educational mission but at its center. Like other church-sponsored educational efforts, adult programs should reflect in their own unique way the three interrelated purposes of Christian education: the teaching of doctrine, the building and experiencing of community, and service to others.

44 It is essential that such programs recognize not only the particular needs of adults, but also their maturity and experience. Those who teach in the name of the Church do not simply instruct adults, but also learn from them; they will only be heard by adults if they listen to them. For this reason adult programs must be planned and conducted in ways that emphasize self-direction, dialogue, and mutual responsibility.

45 There are many instruments of adult education, and the Church itself sponsors many such activities and programs. Their full potential in this area should be recognized and used effectively. The liturgy is one of the most powerful educational instruments at the disposal of the Church. The fact that homilies can be effective tools of adult education lends urgency to current efforts to upgrade preaching skills and to improve the entire homiletic process. The Catholic press and other communications media should be utilized creatively for continuing education.

46 Finally, formal programs of adult education at the parish and diocesan levels deserve adequate attention and support, including professional staffing and realistic funding. Adult education should also have a recognized place in the structure of church-sponsored education at all levels, parish, diocesan and national.

Adult Religious Education

47 The gradual manner of God's self-revelation, manifested in Scripture, is a model for the catechetical efforts of the Church. The full content of revelation can be communicated best to those able by reason of maturity and prior preparation to hear and respond to it. Religious education for adults is the culmination of the entire catechetical effort because it affords an opportunity to teach the whole Christian message. (*General Catechetical Directory,* 20) Catechetics for children and young people should find completion in a catechetical program for adults.

48 The content of such a program will include contemporary sociological and cultural developments considered in the light of faith, current questions concerning religious and moral issues, the relationship of the "temporal" and "ecclesial" spheres of life, and the "rational foundations" of religious belief. (*General Catechetical Directory,* 97) Adult religious education should strive not only to impart instruction to adults but to enable them better to assume responsibility for the building of community and for Christian service in the world.

Education for Family Life

49 Like many institutions in society, the family is under severe pressure today. Challenges to accepted values, changing sexual mores, new ideas about marriage and especially about the sanctity of life—these and other factors can threaten family life and unity.

50 To respond creatively to such pressures and to build a healthy family life, Catholic adults who have assumed or are about to assume the responsibility of marriage must see the family as an image of the Church itself and base their marriage and family life on Christian values taught by the Church in the name of Jesus. As the Church struggles to fulfill Christ's mandate to sanctify and teach men and women in the difficult circumstances of life today, so should a man and a woman, united in marriage and imbued with the Gospel ideal, seek mutual growth in Christ and strive to form, in light of Christian values, the children whom God entrusts to their care. But as all the people of the Church are imperfect human beings who live their vocations imperfectly, so parents approach their vocation conscious of their limitations but aware also that by persevering effort to meet their responsibilities, even in the face of failure and disappointment, they help their children learn what faith, hope and love mean in practice. Finally, as the Church, in imitation of Christ, must constantly seek to be more sensitive and responsive to the needs of the poor among us, so must each Christian family see Christ in those who are less fortunate and, at cost to its own convenience and comfort, strive to be Christ to them, in the parish, the neighborhood, and the larger communities of the nation and world.

51 In seeking to instill this understanding of the Christian family's role, family life education must employ such means as premarital instruction and marriage counseling, study, prayer and action groups for couples, and other adult programs which married persons themselves may plan and conduct in collaboration with Church leadership.

Parents as Educators

52 While it was relatively easy in more stable times for parents to educate their children and transmit their values to them, the immense complexity of today's society makes this a truly awesome task. Without forgetting, then, that parents are "the first to communicate the faith to their children and to educate them," (*Apostolate of the Laity,* 11) the Christian community must make a generous effort today to help them fulfill their duty. This is particularly true in regard to two matters of great sensitivity and importance, religious education and education in human sexuality.

53 Although religious education should foster unity within the family and the Church, today at times it causes division instead.

There are several reasons for this. Changes in religious education in recent years have disturbed many parents, in part at least because the training their children now receive seems to bear little resemblance to their own. To the extent that this problem relates to valid pedagogical methods, it may be resolved as parents come to understand better the techniques of contemporary religious education. However, the difficulty also touches at times on more basic issues involving the orthodoxy and authenticity of what is taught.

54 Religious truth must be communicated in a relevant manner which gives each student a vital experience of faith. But it must also be transmitted fully and accurately. There is no opposition between orthodoxy and relevance. Religious truth is itself supremely relevant, and the manner in which it is presented must make this manifest. The Catholic community today faces the challenge of combining these complementary values—orthodoxy and relevance—in viable programs of religious education for the young. The steps to achieving this cannot be spelled out in the abstract but must instead be worked out in dialogue and cooperation on the parish, diocesan and national levels. Parents, religious educators, including authors and publishers of textbooks, pastors, bishops, must seek together, in a spirit of mutual respect and shared commitment to the values of orthodoxy and relevance, to solve the problems and ease the tensions that now exist. They will find guidance in such sources as the *General Catechetical Directory* issued by the Holy See, "The Basic Teachings of Catholic Religious Education" to be issued by the American bishops, and the projected U.S. national catechetical directory.

55 Continuing education will help parents understand the approach, content and methods of contemporary religious education. At the same time, however, parents must not only be helped to understand the aims and methods of catechesis; they must also be involved in planning and evaluating the catechetical programs provided for their children. (*General Catechetical Directory*, 79) And in order that this evaluation may be realistic and informed, parents and other members of the Christian community have a right to expect at least that the content of these programs will be expressed in doctrinally adequate formulae as an, assurance that the programs are indeed capable of transmitting the authentic Christian message.

56 If neglecting parental involvement can only contribute to further misunderstanding and polarization in catechetics, the same is equally true of the sensitive subject of education in human sexuality. In 1968 we affirmed the "value and necessity of wisely planned education of children in human sexuality" and acknowledged our "grave obligation" to assist parents, who are "primarily responsible for imparting to their children an awareness of the sacredness of sexuality." (*Human Life in Our Day*, 61) We continue to regard this as an important priority in Christian education, met in part through diocesan-approved family life education in Catholic schools and other instructional programs.

57 These efforts presuppose parental understanding and approval and require parents' cooperation with classroom teachers. The aim is not to supplant parents but to help them fulfill their obligation. They have a right to be informed about the content of such programs and to be assured that diocesan-approved textbooks and other instructional materials meet the requirements of propriety. But when these reasonable conditions have been met, parents should not allow continuing anxiety to be translated into indiscriminate opposition to all forms of classroom education in sexuality. Such opposition would be contrary to the teaching of Vatican Council II and the pastoral policy of the American bishops. Also, to the extent that it might disrupt responsible efforts to provide formal education in sexuality for the young, it would violate the rights of other, no less conscientious, parents who ask for such instruction for their own children.

58 The child's need for and right to adequate knowledge and guidance, adapted to his age and individual maturity are the paramount considerations. In all programs proper emphasis must be given to the spiritual and moral dimensions of sexuality. The child's reverence for the God-given dignity and beauty of sex is an effective safeguard of purity; it should be cultivated from the earliest years.

59 These remarks all underline the fact that a "parent component" must be part of many different church-sponsored educational programs. Where appropriate, Catholic schools can offer courses for parents. School-related parent organizations should provide opportunities for adults to learn more about child development and pedagogical method. Similar provision for educating and involving adults should be made by parish religious education programs. All this requires teachers professionally educated for work in this area.

Adult Education and Social Problems

60 "The constant expansion of population, scientific and technical progress, and the tightening of bonds between men have not only immensely widened the field of the lay apostolate . . . These developments have themselves raised new problems which cry out for the skillful concern and attention of the laity." (*Apostolate of the Laity,* 1) Adult education must therefore deal with the critical issues of contemporary society. "The role of the Church today is very difficult; to reconcile man's modern respect for progress with the norms of humanity and of the gospel teaching." (*Mater et Magistra,* 256) Applying the Gospel message to social problems is a delicate but crucial task for which all members of the Church are responsible but which is entrusted in a specific way to lay people.

61 In proclaiming the social doctrine of the Gospel, the aim is not to antagonize but to reconcile. But the proclamation must be forthright, even where forthrightness challenges widely accepted attitudes and practices. Even though Christians may at times err in their facts, interpretations, and conclusions about social issues, they must not fail to apply the Gospel to contemporary life. Adult programs which deal with social problems in light of Gospel values thus have an extremely important place in the Church's educational mission. And, as in other areas of adult education, participants in such programs must be encouraged to bring their insights and experiences to planning and conducting them.

HIGHER EDUCATION

62 While higher education has always been important in the United States, our rapid evolution as a technological society since World War II has given universities and colleges an even more prominent role in American life. Americans look to them for expert knowledge in a multitude of fields and depend on them for many functions which powerfully affect social and economic life. This is reflected in the remarkable growth of college and university enrollment. Today more than half of American young people of college age attend institutions of post-secondary education. The nation should be aware, however, that many private institutions, including Catholic ones, are not now sharing in this growth. For many, rising costs and dependence on tuition have caused a student shortage which threatens their survival.

63 Like the nation, the Church is greatly influenced by higher education and indebted to it in many ways. Cooperation between these two great institutions, Church and university, is indispensable to the health of society.

64 Everything possible must be done to preserve the critically important contribution made by Catholic institutions through their commitment to the spiritual, intellectual, and moral values of the Christian tradition. Their students have a right to explore the distinctively Catholic intellectual patrimony which affirms, among other things, the existence of God and His revelation in Jesus Christ as ontological facts and essential elements in seeking and sharing truth. The Church itself looks to its colleges and universities to serve it by deep and thorough study of Catholic beliefs in an atmosphere of intellectual freedom and according to canons of intellectual criticism which should govern all pursuit of truth. The Catholic community should therefore fully support practical efforts to assure the continued, effective presence of distinctively Catholic colleges and universities in our nation.

65 The same support and concern should be extended to all of higher education. The Church desires a commitment in every college and university to the full and free pursuit and study of truth, including the place of religion in the lives of individuals and society. Catholics are further called to give their support to all of higher education by the fact that the great majority of Catholics who enter college enroll in non-Catholic institutions. These young men and women have a strong claim on the service and affection of the entire Catholic community; among them are many future leaders of the nation and the Church.

Campus Ministry

66 The Second Vatican Council urged all "pastors of the Church" not only to seek the spiritual welfare of students in

Catholic institutions of higher education, but also to ensure that "at colleges and universities which are not Catholic, there are Catholic residences and centers where priests, religious and laymen who have been judiciously chosen and trained can serve on campus as sources of spiritual and intellectual assistance to young people." (*Christian Education,* 10) While the Council's emphasis reflected conditions as they were up to that time, developments since then point to the importance of campus ministry in Catholic institutions as well. These developments include a decline in the number of priests and religious engaged in Catholic higher education, the increasing number of students who have not attended church-sponsored elementary and secondary schools, and some strong pressures to secularize Catholic institutions.

67 Wherever exercised, campus ministry has a number of distinct but related goals. These include promoting theological study and reflection on man's religious nature so that intellectual, moral and spiritual growth can proceed together; sustaining a Christian community on campus with the pastoral care and liturgical worship it requires; integration of its apostolic ministry with other ministries of the local community and the diocese; and helping the Christian community on campus to serve its members and others, including the many non-students who gravitate toward the university. Campus ministry thus involves far more than pastoral care given by chaplains to students. It is pastoral, educational and prophetic, including a complex of efforts to give witness to the Gospel message to all persons within the college or university. It is conducted not only by priests and religious, but also by lay faculty and administrators, students and members of the local community.

68 Among the challenges facing campus ministry today are the special problems posed by "commuter" colleges and universities and the rapidly growing number of two-year colleges, whose enrollment is expected to reach five million by the middle of this decade. Students in these schools differ greatly from students in four-year, largely residential institutions, since most of them live at home and have jobs and many are married.

69 The work of campus ministry requires continual evaluation of traditional methods of ministry and also of new approaches which are licitly and responsibly employed. These latter can be highly appropriate in the campus setting, where there exists an audience receptive to the kind of sound innovation which may in the future prove beneficial to the larger Catholic community.

70 Religious studies, formal or informal, should be part of every campus ministry program. Neglect of such studies would risk a growth in religious indifferentism. Today, when the importance of reason and rational discourse is questioned and frequently slighted in favor of the affective side of life, there is need for emphasis on the relationship of faith and reason.

71 At the same time campus ministry must reflect the fact that young people, while deeply concerned about personal holiness and salvation, also seek meaning and values through the life of community. A community of believers engaged in analysis and practice of their faith is a sign of the continuing vitality of the Church. Such a community is sympathetic to all who search sincerely for the meaning of life and seek a foundation for values which will guide them in the pursuit of their destiny.

72 Campus ministry must have its proper place in the educational and financial planning of every diocese. The selection, preparation and continuing education of the men and women of campus ministry should have a high priority in educational planning. Regional and national programs must be developed to promote the development of campus ministry not only for its own sake but for the sake of increased dialogue between the Church and the university.

Catholic Colleges and Universities

73 The Catholic college or university seeks to give the authentic Christian message an institutional presence in the academic world. Several things follow from this. Christian commitment will characterize this academic community. While fully maintaining the autonomy concomitant to its being a college or university, the institution will manifest fidelity to the teaching of Jesus Christ as transmitted by His Church. The advancement of Christian thought will be the object of institutional commitment. The human sciences will be examined in light of Catholic faith. The best of the Christian intellectual and spiritual tradition will be blended with the special dynamism of contemporary higher education in a way that enriches both.

74 The Catholic college or university must of course be an institution of higher education according to sound contemporary criteria. It will therefore be strongly committed to academic excellence and the responsible academic freedom required for effective teaching and research.

75 For a Catholic institution, there is a special aspect to academic freedom. While natural truth is directly accessible to us by virtue of our innate ability to comprehend reality, the datum or raw material from which theological reflection arises is not a datum of reality fully accessible to human reason. The authentic Christian message is entrusted by Jesus Christ to His community, the Church. Theological research and speculation, which are entirely legitimate and commendable enterprises, deal with divine revelation as their source and material, and the results of such investigation are therefore subject to the judgment of the magisterium.

76 Historically, Catholic colleges and universities have had varying degrees of relationship to ecclesiastical authority. The concern of Vatican Council II with these institutions centered on their nature or function, their faculty, and their role in Christian formation. (*Christian Education,* 10) At present, cordial, fruitful and continuing dialogue on the complex question of the relationship of the Catholic college or university to the Church is proceeding between representatives of such schools and others officially concerned with Catholic education. The entire Catholic community stands to benefit from this continued exploration.

Theology and the Catholic University

77 As an institution committed to examination of the full range of human existence, the university should probe the religious dimension of life. Scholars engaged in theological and religious studies should thus be part of the academic community.

78 A department of theology, conceived and functioning as an integral part of the Catholic university, can encourage scholars in other disciplines to examine more deeply their own fields of study. The theological scholar himself is enriched by participating in such discussion.

79 The department of theology also encourages students to confront religious questions and explore beyond the limits of a narrow vision of life which excludes the religious dimension. At the same time, interaction with students obliges scholars to respond to the healthy challenge of reexamining their insights and modes of expression.

80 Finally, the department of theology is a vital resource to the Catholic community outside the university and must be aware of its responsibility to that community. Its scholarship can provide support to the pastoral ministry of the Church and help deepen the Church's understanding of the Gospel message. Theologians can render special assistance to bishops, whose role, like theirs, includes both the development and the defense of Christian truth.

81 While no aspect of genuine religious experience is beyond the scope of concern of the department of theology or religious studies in a Catholic university, its characteristic strength appropriately lies in the presence of scholars whose professional competence and personal commitment are rooted in the Catholic tradition. In such an institution every scholar, Catholic or not, is also obliged to respect its spirit and purpose.

2. THE EDUCATIONAL MINISTRY TO YOUTH

82 "The future of humanity lies in the hands of those who are strong enough to provide coming generations with reasons for living and hoping." (The Church Today, 31) Here as in other areas of educational ministry the threefold purpose of Christian education provides a guide for developing and evaluating programs. Educational programs for the young must strive to teach doctrine, to do so within the experience of Christian community, and to prepare individuals for effective Christian witness and service to others. In doing this they help foster the student's growth in personal holiness and his relationship with Christ.

83 This ideal of Christian education will best be realized by programs which create the widest opportunities for students to receive systematic catechesis, experience daily living in a faith community, and develop commitment and skill in serving others. All who share responsibility for educational ministry should support programs which give promise of realizing this threefold purpose which is the guide and inspiration of all the Church's educational efforts.

84 The history of American education is testimony to the deeply held conviction of American Catholics that Catholic elementary and secondary schools are the best expression of the educational ministry to youth. As we shall explain at length later, this remains our conviction today, one shared, we believe, by the great majority of American Catholics. Yet we choose to deal here first with religious education programs for children and young people who attend public and other non-Catholic schools not because Catholic schools are any less important than in the past—their importance is in fact greater now than ever before—but because the urgency and the difficulty of the educational ministry to the students outside them warrant this emphasis. Among the pastoral issues in education which today challenge the Catholic community in our nation, none is more pressing than providing Catholic education for these young people.

RELIGIOUS EDUCATION OUTSIDE THE CATHOLIC SCHOOL

85 Confraternity of Christian Doctrine and other parish programs of religious education are essential instruments of catechesis. Besides enrolling some five and a half million students, they have an even larger potential outreach among the many Catholic children and young people who attend neither Catholic schools nor out-of-school religious education programs. These students, both present and potential, are the youth of whom the Second Vatican Council spoke in urging the Catholic community to be "present" to them with its "special affection and helpfulness." (*Christian Education*, 2)

86 Obviously a part-time, out-of-school program of religious education labors under special handicaps in attempting to achieve the threefold purpose of Christian education. Yet we have a grave duty toward the students for whom such programs now represent the only means of formal religious instruction available to them. Parents, educators, and pastors must do all in their power to provide these children and young people with programs which correspond as fully as possible with the ideal of Catholic education.

Doctrine, Community and Service

87 Pastoral programs of religious education for young people outside Catholic schools must be developed and conducted within the framework of the threefold purpose of Christian education. Merely "teaching about" religion is not enough. Instead such programs must strive to teach doctrine fully, foster community, and prepare their students for Christian service. Whether it takes place in a Catholic school or not, it is essential that the Catholic community offer children and young people an experience of catechesis which indeed gives "clarity and vigor" to faith, fosters living in the spirit of Christ, encourages participation in the liturgy and sacraments, and motivates involvement in the apostolate. (*Christian Education,* 4)

88 Although there are inherent limitations in out-of-school programs; there are also considerable strengths which should be recognized and built upon. A limitation, which is also a potential source of strength, is their voluntary character, which, while making it more difficult to secure participation, also offers significant opportunities for the building of Christian community. The fact that participants in leadership, teaching or student roles, are volunteers provides creative planners with opportunity to develop esprit among them, and indeed, to foster a stronger sense of community within the entire parish. This is simply to apply to the out-of-school program what has long been recognized as true of the parish school, namely that the hard work and sacrifice required for success can be powerful forces for Christian fellowship.

89 In regard to service, administrators and teachers in such programs offer personal witness to the meaning of Christian service by their dedicated effort to impart Christian truth and values to the young. This must be carried further, however, by giving the programs themselves an orientation to service of both the parish community and the community outside the parish. For service is itself an efficacious means of teaching doctrine, and thus these programs should include opportunities for service as part of the educational experience they seek to provide the young. Today, when many people have more leisure time than in the past, it is appropriate that a parish increasingly turn its attention to the task of preparing its members, young and old, for service within and beyond the Christian community,

90 In many places pastoral programs of religious education are now demonstrating vitality and effectiveness in achieving the threefold purpose of Christian education, especially in parishes which are true communities of faith. Their success deserves recognition, praise and imitation. The achievements of some innovative and imaginative programs for high school students offer a bright ray of hope in a particularly difficult area. Some parishes have made substantial progress in becoming centers for the religious education of all parishioners, young and old. In short, there now exist across the nation a variety of successful models which should be studied and translated into similar efforts elsewhere.

Problems and Policies

91 Despite their achievements and bright hopes, such programs face serious problems which should concern the entire Catholic community. These programs do not reach large numbers of Catholic young people not in Catholic schools. Many of them may simply not be accessible or receptive to any systematic, organized program of religious education now available to the Church. There are many reasons for this: parental indifference; problems of scheduling; pressures of time; demands on and appeals to their loyalty by other communities of which they are members; the inadequacy of some religious education programs, an inadequacy often due to insufficient financing and reliance on personnel who have not had proper training and support. But practical difficulties, frustrations and disappointments accentuate the need for the Catholic community to increase its effort in this crucial area. As a matter of policy, religious education programs for Catholic students who attend public and other non-Catholic schools should receive high priority everywhere, a priority expressed in adequate budgets and increased service from professional religious educators. In this light we offer the following pastoral guidelines.

Guidelines for the Future

92 The essential unity of the educational ministry should be reflected in its programmatic expressions. The educational mission of the Church is one. It takes form in many institutions, programs and activities which, different as they are, all derive inspiration, rationale and purpose from the same source: the one educational mission of the Church which is essentially a continuation in our times of the mission of Jesus Christ. Far from competing with one another for money, personnel, students, etc., they must function together harmoniously and efficiently, complementing and supplementing one another in order to achieve jointly the fullest possible realization of the threefold aim of Christian education: teaching doctrine, building community, and serving others.

93 Since religious education programs for Catholic students who do not attend Catholic schools are an essential part of the Church's total educational ministry, their staff and students should be integrated fully into the unified educational ministry of the local Christian community. In parishes this calls for efforts to draw together these programs and the Catholic schools in closer working relationships: for example, by including "CCD" students in school and parish organizations and activities to the greatest extent possible, and, in parishes which have no schools, by doing the same for students who attend Catholic schools outside the parish. The objective—integration of all pastoral and educational programs into a unified whole whose components complement and assist one another—should be a major concern of parish leadership. In this regard, consideration should be given to common funding of all catechetical education in a parish for both the school and out-of-school programs.

94 Parishes which have Catholic schools should explore new ways of placing them more directly at the service of the entire parish community. The school should be a focal point for many educational efforts on behalf of children, young people, and adults. Where there is no parish school a parish educational center should serve the same function of drawing together programs and people.

95 Where a parish school must be closed, there should be careful advance planning to provide funds and personnel for such a center.

96 Parishes without parochial schools must not limit their programs to the bare essentials of religious instruction. Their children and young people deserve Catholic education in as full a sense as possible. This suggests that traditional programs be enriched with a variety of informal experiences to help pupils discover the meaning of Christian community life and its potential for service to others. New study and effort are needed to utilize communications media and modern technology in religious education. In areas where parishes and missions confront the problems of isolation and limited resources, regional catechetical centers, either drawing together students from a broad geographical area or sending out teams of skilled catechists into the parishes of the region, may help meet the need for high quality, comprehensive religious education. In short, far from being an excuse for an inferior program, the absence of a parochial school simply challenges a parish, either alone or in cooperation with other parishes, to expand its efforts to give its children and young people as broad a Catholic educational experience as it possibly can.

97 The effectiveness of voluntary service in religious education programs must be strengthened. Parish leadership should give recognition and moral support to the volunteers engaged in this work, but, more than that, it should provide adequately financed opportunities for their professional preparation and in-service training. Furthermore, these programs, while retaining their distinctive voluntarism, must at the same time be reinforced by the increased use of well trained, adequately paid professionals in key positions. Organizations which serve the professional needs of personnel working in this field should receive official recognition and encouragement.

98 Careful attention should be given to providing religious education for members of minority groups and to involving them in the mainstream of the catechetical effort.

99 The right of the handicapped to receive religious education adapted to their special needs also challenges the ingenuity and commitment of the Catholic community.

100 Planning is essential to create a unified system of religious education accessible and attractive to all the People of God. We must continue to explore new ways of extending the educational ministry to every Catholic child and young person. In doing so, we must be open to the possibility of new forms and structures for all Catholic education in the years ahead. With regard to the "tasks and responsibilities" of catechesis, "it is not enough to rest content with the distribution of forces already existing; it is also necessary that effort on the part of all Christians be more and more stimulated and promoted. Care must be taken to make the Christian community every day conscious of its duty." (*General Catechetical Directory*, 107) A comprehensive vision of the Christian ministry in education, and integrated structures to embody it, seem now to offer the best hope for achieving the greatest success with the largest number of Catholic children and young people, both those who attend Catholic schools and those who do not.

CATHOLIC SCHOOLS

101 Of the educational programs available to the Catholic community, Catholic schools afford the fullest and best opportunity to realize the threefold purpose of Christian education among children and young people. Schools naturally enjoy educational advantages which other programs either cannot offer or can offer only with great difficulty. A school has a greater claim on the time and loyalty of the student and his family. It makes more accessible to students participation in the liturgy and the sacraments, which are powerful forces for the development of personal sanctity and for the building of community. It provides a more favorable pedagogical and psychological environment for teaching Christian faith. With the Second Vatican Council we affirm our conviction that the Catholic school "retains its immense importance in the circumstances of our times" and we recall the duty of Catholic parents "to entrust their children to Catholic schools, when and where this is possible, to support such schools to the extent of their ability, and to work along with them for the welfare of their children." (*Christian Education,* 8)

Doctrine, Community, Service

102 Christian education is intended to "make men's faith become living, conscious, and active, through the light of instruction." (*The Bishops' Office in the Church,* 14) The Catholic school is the unique setting within which this ideal can be realized in the lives of Catholic children and young people.

103 Only in such a school can they experience learning and living fully integrated in the light of faith. The Catholic school "strives to relate all human culture eventually to the news of salvation, so that the life of faith will illumine the knowledge which students gradually gain of the world, of life, and of mankind." (*Christian Education, 8*) Here, therefore, students are instructed in human knowledge and skills, valued indeed for their own worth but seen simultaneously as deriving their most profound significance from God's plan for His creation. Here, too, instruction in religious truth and values is an integral part of the school program. It is not one more subject alongside the rest, but instead it is perceived and functions as the underlying reality in which the student's experiences of learning and living achieve their coherence and their deepest meaning.

104 This integration of religious truth and values with the rest of life is brought about in the Catholic school not only by its unique curriculum but, more important, by the presence of teachers who express an integrated approach to learning and living in their private and professional lives. It is further reinforced by free interaction among the students themselves within their own community of youth.

105 This integration of religious truth and values with life distinguishes the Catholic school from other schools. This is a matter of crucial importance today in view of contemporary trends and pressures to compartmentalize life and learning and to isolate the religious dimension of existence from other areas of human life. A Catholic for whom religious commitment is the central, integrative reality of his life will find in the Catholic school a perception and valuation of the role of religion which matches his own.

106 More than any other program of education sponsored by the Church, the Catholic school has the opportunity and obligation to be unique, contemporary, and oriented to Christian service: unique because it is distinguished by its commitment to the threefold purpose of Christian education and by its total design and operation which foster the integration of religion with the rest of learning and living; contemporary because it enables students to address with Christian insight the multiple problems which face individuals and society today; oriented to Christian service because it helps students acquire skills, virtues, and habits of heart and mind required for effective service to others. All those involved in a Catholic school—parents, pastors, teachers, administrators, and students—must earnestly desire to make it a community of faith which is indeed "living, conscious, and active."

107 The program of studies in a Catholic school reflects the importance which the school and sponsoring community attach to Christian formation. Basic to this task, as we have said earlier, is instruction which is authentic in doctrine and contemporary in presentation. Failure on either side renders the instruction ineffective and can in fact impede the growth of living faith in the child. Thus the proper use of new catechetical methods designed with these objectives in view is to be applauded, as are many new programs for the professional development of religion teachers. They can contribute to making Catholic schools true communities of faith in which the formational efforts of Catholic families are complemented, reinforced and extended. Within such communities teachers and pupils experience together what it means to live a life of prayer, personal responsibility and freedom reflective of Gospel values. Their fellowship helps them grow in their commitment to service of God, one another, the Church, and the general community.

108 Building and living community must be prime, explicit goals of the contemporary Catholic school. Community is an especially critical need today largely because natural communities of the past have been weakened by many influences. Pressures on the family, the basic unit of society, have already been noted. Urbanization and suburbanization have radically changed the concept of neighborhood community.

109 Racial and ethnic tensions and other conflicts reflect an absence of local and national community. War and the exploitation of poor nations by the rich dramatize the same tragic lack of community on the international level. Today's Catholic school must respond to these challenges by developing in its students a commitment to community and to the social skills and virtues needed to achieve it. Participation together in the liturgy and in paraliturgical activities and spiritual exercises can effectively foster community among students and faculty. Since the Gospel spirit is one of peace, brotherhood, love, patience and respect for others, a school rooted in these principles ought to explore ways to deepen its students' concern for and skill in peacemaking and the achievement of justice. Here young people can learn together of human needs, whether in the parish, the neighborhood, the local civic community, or the world, and begin to respond to the obligation of Christian service through joint action.

110 At the level of institutional commitment, too, service of the public interest is a notable quality of Catholic and other non-public schools in America. "Private education has played and is playing a significant and valuable role in raising national levels of knowledge, competence and experience." (Justice Byron White in Board of Education v. Allen [392 U.S. 236]) Countless men and women have been better able to contribute to the political, social and economic life of the nation as a result of their education in nonpublic schools. This service has been extended not only to those already in the mainstream of social life, but also to many suffering special disadvantages, including in a notable way the physically and mentally handicapped.

111 Other benefits flow from the private educational effort into the lifeblood of the nation. These schools supply a diversity which the American educational system would otherwise lack. They provide desirable competition for the public schools, not as antagonists, but as partners in the total American educational enterprise. In a unique way they serve the community by keeping viable the right to freedom of choice under law among educational alternatives. Most important, the commitment of Catholic schools to Christian values and the Christian moral code renders a profound service to society which depends on spiritual values and good moral conduct for its very survival.

The Crisis of Catholic Schools

112 It will perhaps be objected that much of what has been said up to now paints an ideal picture of the Catholic school and its purposes. Truly it is an ideal, but little is achieved without ideals to strive for. Furthermore, Catholic schools have realized and continue to realize this ideal more successfully than is sometimes acknowledged today.

113 Of the Catholic school in America we say humbly, and with gratitude for the grace of God manifested in it, that it has nurtured the faith of Jesus Christ in millions of men and women who have lived vibrantly Christian lives and have given themselves generously in service to others. Scarcely a man or woman in the Church in America today has not benefited either directly or indirectly from the sacrifices of his fellow Christians in creating the Catholic school system. A full measure of gratitude is due to the dedicated teachers who have expressed their Christian vocation through the apostolate of Catholic education. All deserve the thanks of the Catholic community, especially the religious women whose resourceful leadership has been at the heart of the Catholic school effort in the United States throughout its history.

114 Today this school system is shrinking visibly. The reasons are many and include complex sociological, demographic and psychological factors. Some believe there has been an excessive effort in formal education and too much concentration on schools at the expense of other educational programs. Some are convinced that other forms of Christian service take unequivocal priority over service rendered in the classroom. Some feel American Catholics no longer have the material resources to support so ambitious an educational enterprise.

115 Financial problems have contributed significantly to the present crisis. Burdened by the spiraling costs of both public and nonpublic education, those who support nonpublic schools have placed their cause before their fellow Americans. While legislators have responded in many instances, courts have often rejected laws favorable to nonpublic education, sometimes on grounds which many find extremely difficult to understand or accept.

116 The chief obstacle to meaningful public aid to nonpublic elementary and secondary schools continues to be the United States Supreme Court's interpretation of the First and Fourteenth Amendments. The Court, however, has decided only the cases brought before it; it has not rendered judgment on every conceivable plan. To some it appears that the Court has raised an impenetrable barrier between government and church-sponsored schools; but to others, who are knowledgeable about its jurisprudence and procedures, it appears that the Court, having acknowledged that it is walking a tightrope between the First Amendment's free exercise and establishment clauses, may eventually see a way to give realistic support to parents' freedom to choose a nonpublic school.

117 The words of Pope Pius XI, written some 40 years ago in the encyclical on Christian education, afford timely encouragement to those seeking justice for Catholic schools. "Catholics will never feel, whatever may have been the sacrifices already made, that they have done enough, for the support and defense of their schools and for the securing of laws that will do them justice." (*Christian Education of Youth*)

118 We are well aware of the problems which now face the Catholic school system in the United States. We also wish our position to be clear. For our part, as bishops, we reaffirm our conviction that Catholic schools which realize the threefold purpose of Christian education—to teach doctrine, to build community, and to serve—are the most effective means available to the Church for the education of children and young people who thus may "grow into manhood according to the mature measure of Christ." (*Christian Education*, 2; cf. Ephesians, 4:13) We call upon all members of the Catholic community to do everything in their power to maintain and strengthen Catholic schools which embrace the threefold purpose of Christian education.

Action Needed Now

119 Specific steps can and should be taken now by concerned parents, educators, pastors and others to ensure the continuance and improvement of Catholic schools. (Cf. for example, *Nonpublic Schools and the Public Good,* Final Report: The President's Panel on Nonpublic Education)

120 These will include such things as stating clearly and compellingly the distinctive goals of the Catholic school; increasing associations with other nonpublic and public schools; practicing fiscal, professional, academic and civic accountability; conducting vigorous programs of student recruitment; joining with other nonpublic schools in public relations efforts; exercising firm control over operating costs and practicing greater efficiency in the use of facilities and personnel; intensifying efforts to increase income from private sources, including those which have generally gone untapped up to now; entering into partnership with institutions of higher learning; undertaking school consolidations at the elementary and secondary levels where circumstances make this educationally desirable; and participating fully in the search for solutions to the racial crisis in American education.

121 The unfinished business on the agenda of Catholic schools, like many other schools, also includes the task of providing quality education for the poor and disadvantaged of our nation. Generous, sustained sacrifice is demanded of those whom God has favored in order to make available educational programs which meet the need of the poor to be self-determining, free persons in all areas of individual and social life. Recognition of past failures should not obscure the fact that the Church in many places does provide a wide variety of services for the poor, including schools of high quality, often at the cost of heroic sacrifice and with encouraging success. What is now being accomplished, however, should serve only as a spur to renewed commitment and continued effort in this area so crucial to the good of society and so central to the mission of the Church.

122 If the Catholic community is convinced of the values and advantages of Catholic schools, it must and will act now to adopt such measures and face such challenges as these. In particular all those involved in the Catholic school effort should avoid a defeatist attitude which would regard present problems as a prelude to disaster. Difficult as they may be, they are not insoluble, given the will and the intelligence to seek and adopt solutions.

Catholic Schools Called to Reorganization

123 Like other schools in our nation, Catholic schools are called to a renewal of purpose, and some to reorganization. The goals appropriate to today's Catholic educational effort, and thus to today's Catholic schools, are in some ways more challenging than in the past, including as they do the need to prepare young men and women to be witnesses to faith during an era of instability and at the same time to act as agents of creative institutional change for which adequate models hardly exist. While the Christian purpose of the Catholic school must always be clearly evident, no one form is prescribed for it.

124 The search for new forms of schooling should therefore continue. Some may bear little resemblance to schooling as we have known it: the parish education center; the family education center; the school without walls, drawing extensively on community resources; the counseling center; etc. We do not mention these new forms to canonize what some may regard as educational fads or to presume a kind of knowledge we do not possess. The point is that one must be open to the possibility that the school of the future, including the Catholic school, will in many ways be very different from the school of the past. Consideration should also be given to the relationship of parish and school where circumstances suggest that the traditional parish may no longer provide the best framework for formal schooling.

125 New forms require pilot programs along with study and evaluation. Catholic schools have the capacity and freedom to experiment. Administrators and teachers should therefore cooperate with parents in designing experimental models or pilot programs to improve educational standards and results.

126 Reorganization may also involve new models of sponsorship and collaboration. Various forms of cooperation with public schools should be explored. In supporting a school system which provides an alternative to the system sponsored by the state, the Catholic community does not wish to ignore or be isolated from public schools. On all levels of education, and particularly on a system-wide basis, Catholic educators should seek actively to cooperate with their public school counterparts and their colleagues in other nonpublic schools, sharing ideas, plans, personnel, technology, and other resources where mutually feasible and beneficial. The possibility of institutional cooperation with other Christian groups in the field of education should be explored. Approached with candor and intelligence, cooperative planning need not threaten the identity or independence of any school system and can benefit all.

YOUTH MINISTRY

127 Youth ministry today faces challenges created by the problems and needs of youth in our society. Mirroring to a great extent the alienation and uncertainty of adults, many young people in this country, as well as in other nations of the world, feel estranged both from traditional values and from an adult society whose actions often belie its own professed commitment to these values. These young people grope for the deeper meaning of life and for roles consonant with their sense of human dignity. The Christian community should be anxious to understand the causes of their uncertainty and eager to respond to what is often an unvoiced cry for help.

128 Other young people, more positively oriented toward society, exhibit encouraging energy and optimism. But even many of them feel unrest and apathy as a result of a socially imposed prolonged adolescence during which they are impeded in their growth to adulthood and frustrated in their efforts to act as responsible persons.

129 Disenchantment with organized religion is often part of the the alienation of the young today. This seems in many instances not to be disenchantment with God or with the spiritual dimension of life but with some institutional forms and functions. Even as society grows more secularistic, many young people, reflecting genuine religious concern, express growing interest in Jesus Christ. Their quest for authentic values by which to live has urgency and commendable authenticity.

130 Christians should be sensitive and discerning in their approach to the young, who through their Baptism and Confirmation have been incorporated into full membership in the Christian community. This community does have solutions to many of the questions which trouble today's youth, but it cannot realistically expect young people to accept them unless it, for its part, is willing to listen to their problems. Thus it must strive not only to teach the young but to learn from them and to see its own institutions through their eyes and to make prudent changes which this insight may suggest.

131 There are thus three distinct tasks for the ministry to youth: to enable young people to take part in the Church's mission to the world in ways appropriate to their age and responsive to their interests; to give a specific dimension—education in service—to religious education; and to interpret young people, their problems and their concerns to the Christian and general communities.

132 Youth have a right and duty to be active participants in the work of the Church in the world. Obviously, however, they face certain obstacles because they are young and lack experience, organizational skills, and other necessary abilities. Adults engaged in youth ministry therefore should function mainly as guides and helpers by giving young people direction and support.

133 Those engaged in youth ministry are by that fact involved in religious education. Their efforts complement the formal religious education carried on in Catholic schools and out-of-school programs. They bring a specific focus to the work of religious education, namely, education for mission. This is done through programs which provide young people with opportunity to engage in action projects exemplifying what it means to be a Christian in the world today. Such projects should be designed and conducted in a way that helps youth see their participation as a true expression of Christian concern and not simply as a natural response to human needs.

134 The youth ministry should also provide for another educational need of the young, education in community. As maturing Christians, young people need to experience a wide variety of communities. They particularly need the experience of being in a community which brings together young people from both Catholic and public schools. Youth programs under Church sponsorship should base their concept of "community" upon the Gospel values proclaimed by Jesus Christ.

135 Among the major responsibilities of a diocesan youth director and others engaged in youth ministry is that of interpreting youth and advocating their legitimate causes to the Christian community and to other communities to which the young belong. Their informal and immediate contact with the young often gives those engaged in youth work a deep insight into the needs and concerns of youth. It is appropriate that they share these concerns with other adults and plead youth's cause with them.

136 Finally, all those involved in Catholic youth work should recognize the value of what is called peer group ministry. Young people themselves "must become the first and immediate apostles to youth exercising their apostolate among themselves and through themselves." (*Apostolate of the Laity,* 12) Young people should be welcomed as co-workers in this genuinely prophetic form of education, and programs which develop their leadership talents should have a central place in the youth ministry.

IV. PLANNING THE EDUCATIONAL MISSION

137 This pastoral message has stressed the need of many different educational programs and institutions and insisted that each is an important part of the total educational ministry. This may seem of questionable value at a time when the material resources available to the Church for education are limited and, perhaps, diminishing. But only if the Catholic community of our nation is fully aware of and committed to various elements of the educational ministry is it likely to provide the resources which are needed. The cooperation of all is vital if the vision sketched here is to be a reality now or in the future.

138 While it is difficult to define and plan the Church's educational mission in this period of rapid institutional change, the effort must continue. Educational needs must be clearly identified; goals and objectives must be established which are simultaneously realistic and creative; programs consistent with these needs and objectives must be designed carefully, conducted efficiently and evaluated honestly.

139 Under the leadership of the Ordinary and his priests, planning and implementing the educational mission of the Church must involve the entire Catholic community. Representative structures and processes should be the normative means by which the community, particularly Catholic parents, addresses fundamental questions about educational needs, objectives, programs and resources. Such structures and processes, already operating in many dioceses and parishes in the United States, should become universal.

140 Vatican Council II urged the establishment of agencies by which the laity can "express their opinion of things which concern the good of the Church." (*Constitution on the Church*, 37) One such agency, long a part of the American experience and in recent years increasingly widespread in Catholic education, is the representative board of education, which, acting on behalf of the community it serves, seeks patiently and conscientiously to direct the entire range of educational institutions and programs within the educational ministry.

141 On the diocesan level, the educational mission can best be coordinated by a single board of education concerned with the needs of the entire local church. Many such boards have already been established and are now rendering important service to the Church and education. They work best when they are broadly representative of all the people of the diocese, laity, priests and religious. Membership should be open to people of many points of view, including those who may perceive needs and advocate approaches different from those expressed in this pastoral.

142 Participatory approaches to decision making are desirable not only in regard to educational policy but in the entire area of pastoral need. Although the Ordinary has ultimate responsibility for coordinating pastoral programs in the diocese, a significant role in setting priorities can be played by the diocesan pastoral council, itself a structure strongly recommended by Vatican II. (*The Bishops' Pastoral Office in the Church,* 27)

143 Much progress has already been made in educational planning by the Church in the United States. Many dioceses and institutions, for example, have sponsored valuable educational research carried out by professional agencies. Sharing the results of these studies through a national clearinghouse would make it easier to exchange data, provide guidance for new studies, help avoid duplication, and assist planning.

AN INVITATION TO COOPERATION

144 The planning and collaboration invited here will only come about through the active cooperation of all involved in the educational apostolate. We especially seek the collaboration of the teachers—priests, religious, and laity—who serve in Catholic schools and other educational programs. If the threefold purpose of Christian education is to be realized, it must be through their commitment to give instruction to their students, to build community among them, and to serve them. Furthermore, teachers bring insights and experience to planning the total educational mission of the Church. We invite and urge their creative contribution to the effort of the entire community to meet the current challenges.

145 The involvement of religious men and women in educational ministry has long provided example and support to the Christian community. They are publicly identified as persons committed to giving witness to Gospel values, notably the value of community. The stability which religious communities have brought to the apostolate has made it possible to continue many schools and programs which could hardly have survived otherwise. Their witness, always valuable, is needed more than ever today. The entire Church will be enriched by authentic renewal of religious communities. All Catholics look forward to their continued presence as a vital force in the total teaching mission of the Church.

146 The number of religious teachers, upon whom Catholic education has historically depended, is declining at present. The entire Catholic community should seek to understand the causes of this phenomenon and should adopt appropriate measures in an attempt to reverse the trend. Clarification of the ecclesial role of women could be a factor in the solution of the much deplored vocations crisis among religious communities of women.

147 A continuing shortage of religious teachers now is one of those signs of the times which Catholics must confront realistically in carrying on the educational ministry. It emphasizes the fact that reliance on lay persons in the work of Catholic education will not only continue in the years ahead but will certainly increase. This is not to suggest, however, that the presence of lay teachers and administrators in Catholic schools and other educational programs is merely a stopgap. They are full partners in the Catholic educational enterprise, and the dramatic increase of their numbers and influence in recent years is welcome and desirable in itself. As with religious, so with lay teachers and administrators, the Catholic community invites not only their continued service but also their increased participation in planning and decision making and their continued emergence in leadership roles.

148 It is also imperative that the Catholic community collaborate with all Americans committed to educational freedom. The right of parents to exercise genuine freedom of choice in education in ways consistent with the principles of justice and equality must be recognized and made operative. In this connection one must hope that our nation will arrive at a satisfactory accommodation on the role of religion in public education, one which respects the rights and legitimate interests of all parents and students.

149 While steps must be taken to ensure legitimate freedom of choice in education for all, special attention should be given to extending it to those in our country who suffer most from educational disadvantage. Efforts at educational self-determination already undertaken by some members of such groups are truly a significant manifestation of man's struggle to be free, akin to the Catholic community's historic effort to be free to direct its educational destiny. Incompatible with such freedom is a philosophy which would demand, in effect, that all educational efforts be subsumed in one educational system. In an area so intimately related to fundamental human needs and rights as is education, coercive theory or practice which results in the elimination of viable educational alternatives is intolerable, however it may be rationalized.

150 The development of Catholic education in this country up to now reflects the religious freedom which Catholics enjoy in the United States. For its part the Catholic community has a long tradition of cooperating with public authoritiy in promoting civic interests in many fields including education. Thus it is important that persons in government and public service, who influence and regulate the educational activities of the state, understand our convictions about what church-sponsored, faith-inspired education contributes to the general good of the nation.

V. A MINISTRY OF HOPE

151 This pastoral document is not the final word on Christian education. In a sense the final word has already been spoken by Jesus Christ whose mission the Christian community continues today in many ways, including the educational ministry. In another sense the final word will never be spoken; it is the task of each generation of Christians to assess their own times and carry on the mission of Christ by means suited to the needs and opportunities they perceive.

152 The educational mission is not exhausted by any one program or institution. By their complementary functions and co-operative activities all programs and institutions contribute to the present realization of the Church's educational mission. All should remain open to new forms, new programs, new methods which give promise of fuller realization of this mission in the future.

153 The educational mission is not directed to any single group within the Christian community or mankind. All have a role to play; all should have a voice in planning and directing.

154 Like the mission and message of Jesus Christ, the Church's educational mission is universal—for all men, at all times, in all places. In our world and in our nation, the mission of Christian education is of critical importance. The truth of Jesus Christ must be taught; the love of Jesus Christ must be extended to persons who seek and suffer.

155 The Christian community has every reason for hope in confronting the challenge of educational ministry today. To all our efforts we join prayer for God's help, and for the intercession of Mary, the Mother of Jesus. We face problems; so did those who came before us, and so will those who follow. But as Christians we are confident of ultimate success, trusting not in ourselves, but in Jesus Christ, who is at once the inspiration, the content, and the goal of Christian education: "the way, and the truth, and the life."

STUDY QUESTIONS

(Numbers refer to paragraph numbers, not pages)

PREFACE

What are the values of consultation? To the person consulted? To the person doing the consulting?   (1)

What is meant by a "ministry" within the Church?   (2)

What does the expression "educational ministry" mean to you?   (2)

By whom is educational ministry exercised?   (2)

What educational areas are included in the scope of this Pastoral? Why not all?   (3)

What problem does the Pastoral hope to clarify? How does it hope to accomplish this?   (4)

Is it possible for a document like this to be the "final word" on its subject? Why?   (4)

CHAPTER I

What are the objectives of Catholic education?   (7)

What help does the Pastoral give for measuring the success or failure of the educational ministry?   (8-10)

Does your experience tend to make you optimistic or pessimistic about the effects of sin upon the individual and society?   (9)

What are some of the Gospel interpretations of the dignity and freedom of each person?   (10)

Do you see ways of applying Gospel values to questions of justice vs injustice?   (11)

Vatican II calls on us to discern the signs of the times. What is meant by the term "discern?"   (10-11)

What good is doctrine if it does not influence conduct?   (10-12)

What do you think St. Paul means when he says, "Let us profess the truth in love?"   (12-20)

How can the Christian community serve the community of the nation? The community of all men on earth?   (13)

How can each person serve the community of the Church?   (10-13)

Are prayer and worship truly forms of service?   (10-14)

Why do American Catholics have a responsibility for peace and justice in other lands?   (11)

Would you be willing to sacrifice some of the comforts of our way of life, or pay more for them, in order to help people in other lands live a more human life? (11)

Why is fellowship in the Holy Spirit the foundation of real community? (12-19)

Why is it impossible to separate personal growth from community growth in the Church? (13)

How do the sacraments reflect and foster community? (14-17)

How does a consideration of the three interlocking dimensions of the educational ministry of the Church open new avenues? (14-32)

What does the fact that "community is at the heart of Christian education" say to a family? (22-25)

How is experiencing community a teaching/learning activity? Is it a religious experience? (22-26)

Community implies service. Is this the service of God? Of man? Of both? (27-30)

CHAPTER II

How should a Christian respond to present-day technological progress? (33-35)

What are the possible effects of technology on man's faith in God? (36-39)

Do you think that technology and material progress make life more truly human, or do you think they are an obstacle to this? (40-41)

CHAPTER III

Why must adults continue life-long efforts to learn? Is this true in religious education? (43)

Are twelve years of the study of religion enough? (43)

In what respect can the Church be considered an image of family life? (49-50)

Parents are the first and most important teachers. Explain their role as educators. (52-59)

What is the meaning of the word "catechetics?" How would catechetical approaches to adults differ from those to children? (55)

What are some of the conditions of modern life which make it imperative that adult religious education be a lifelong experience? (57-60)

How do adult learning methods differ from those of children? (59)

What opportunities do Christian adults have to continue their ministry of education in society? What responsibilities? (60-61)

"Applying the Gospel message to social problems is a delicate but crucial task for which all members of the Church are responsible." What are some of these problems as you see them in your community? (61)

Do you have an adult education program in your parish? How could you go about getting such a program started or improving an existing program? (61)

Why should the Church concern itself with the good health of all higher education? (62)

What are the ways in which higher education contributes to the Church? (62-65)

Why should we have Catholic colleges and universities? (64-65)

What is involved in campus ministry? (66-67)

Why is campus ministry more than the care that chaplains offer to students? (67)

Who should be involved in campus ministry? (67)

How should campus ministry be supported? (72)

How does campus ministry relate to parish life? (71-72)

How can parish ministry and campus ministry help each other? (72)

What are the prime responsibilities of Catholic universities and colleges with regard to: a) freedom to seek the truth, b) fidelity to the truth of Jesus Christ? (73-76)

Are the above-named responsibilities opposed to each other? Explain. (73-76)

What role does the department of theology play in the university? (77-81)

What can be done for the approximately six and one-half million Catholic children and youth who are not enrolled in Catholic schools or CCD programs? (85)

The Pastoral states that merely "teaching about" religion is not sufficient. Since 1963, the U.S. Supreme Court has permitted teaching about religion in the public schools. Discuss the meaning of both statements.

What practical steps must be taken to give religious education programs for Catholic students who attend public schools and other non-Catholic schools the high priority which the Pastoral calls a matter of policy? (86)

Do you feel there are other limitations to out-of-school programs of religious education besides those suggested by the Pastoral? (85-90)

What is the educational mission of the Church? (92)

In what ways can the entire Catholic community become involved in providing Christian education for youngsters in public schools? (91-100)

The educational ministry of the Church is one. Explain how the Catholic school and the out-of-school religious education components of a total parish religious education program can complement and assist each other. (92-93)

What is meant by the assertion that Catholic schools help bring about the integration of religious truth with the rest of life. (93)

Discuss the statement about the "common funding" of all catechetical activity in a parish for *both* parish schools and out-of-school programs. (93-95)

Is the "desire to serve" the prime requisite for a teacher in out-of-school programs of religious education? (93-97)

How can the effectiveness of voluntary service in religious education programs be strengthened? (96)

What integrated structures are needed to offer the best hope of success for the Catholic education of the largest number of Catholic youth? (97-99)

The Pastoral states that "of the educational opportunities available to the Catholic community, Catholic schools afford the fullest and best opportunity to realize the threefold purpose of Christian education among children and young people." How are Catholic schools better prepared to provide those opportunities? (101)

Discuss the following statement from the Pastoral: "With the Second Vatican Council we affirm our conviction that the Catholic school 'retains its immense importance in the circumstances of our times' and we recall the duty of Catholic parents 'to entrust their children to Catholic schools, when and where this is possible, to support such schools to the extent of their ability, and to work along with them for the welfare of their children.' " (101)

Why is it important that religious instruction in the Catholic schools be both authentic and contemporary in presentation? (104)

How does the function of the Catholic school in "building and living community" meet especially crucial needs in today's society? (106)

What should be the relation of Catholic schools to public and other nonpublic schools? (111)

How do Catholic and other nonpublic schools contribute to the public interests? (107-111)

How strong is your commitment to the Catholic schools? Are you willing to take the trouble to persuade legislators of the value of freedom of choice? (111-115)

How would you rate the possibility of some form of public assistance to nonpublic schools? (115-116)

How is the entire Catholic community to be involved in making basic decisions concerning Catholic education?   (106-116)

Discuss the possible steps suggested in the Pastoral for action to ensure the continuance and development of Catholic schools.   (113-116)

What is the role of the Catholic community in improving the understanding of public officials of the contribution of church-sponsored education to the general good of the nation?   (116)

Considering the service function of the Catholic schools described in the Pastoral, what can these schools realistically do to bring quality education to the poor and disadvantaged?   (122)

What steps might you take to ensure the continuance of Catholic schools?   (119-120)

How are the Catholic schools uniquely fitted to the role of searching out new educational forms to respond to the challenges of a changing society?   (124)

What is the recommended framework of consultation and planning for the development of new forms of education in the Catholic schools? (125-126)

What are some of the traditional values many youth seem to question?   (127-129)

What are some ways in which the Christian community may assist the young in their groping for the deeper meaning of life?   (130)

What is "socially imposed prolonged adolescence"? How can we assist youth in their development into adulthood?   (131-134)

Why are many young people disenchanted with organized religion? (129)

What roles might young people take in the teaching mission of the Church?   (132)

What does it mean "to enable young people to take part in the Church's mission to the world in ways appropriate to their age and interests"?   (134)

In what ways can we assist youth in their need for community? How does the adult's need for community differ from youth's? Why? (135-136)

Does your parish have youth on its parish council?

Define "peer group" ministry. What role should adults take in this form of ministry?   (136)

CHAPTER IV

In your opinion what are the most serious threats to the continuance

47

of Catholic schools? What would be the most serious results if they went out of existence?   (144-147)

What is the "ecclesial role" of women?   (146)

CHAPTER V

Discuss the reasons for hope regarding the mission of Christian education.   (152-155)

SUMMARY QUESTIONS

In what ways do you feel that this pastoral might be helpful to you?

What sections of this document would you recommend be further developed for particular application?

INDEX

50